D1490617

THE JOY OF FUNDRAISING

THE JOY OF FUNDRAISING

by Terry Axelrod

How to stop suffering and
start enjoying asking for money
for your favorite cause

PROPERTY OF

MAR – 6 2007

THE FOUNDATION CTR

The Joy of Fundraising: How to Stop Suffering and
Start Enjoying Asking for Money for Your Favorite Cause
Terry Axelrod

Benevon (formerly Raising More Money) Publications, Seattle, Washington
The following trademarks appear throughout this book:
Benevon™, Benevon Model™, Treasure Map®, Point of Entry®,
Free One-Hour Ask Event™, Essential Story™, Visionary Leader™,
Bless and Release™, Table Captains™, Multiple-Year Giving Society™,
Multiple-Year Donors™, Units of Service™, Five-Step Follow-Up Call™.

All text and illustrations © in whole or in part 2006 Terry Axelrod.

Printed and bound in the United States of America. All rights reserved.
No part of this book may be reproduced or transmitted in any form or by any
means, electronic or mechanical, including photocopying, recording, or by
an information storage and retrieval system—except by a reviewer who may
quote brief passages in a review to be printed in a magazine, newspaper,
or on the Web—without permission in writing from the publisher.
For information, please contact:
Benevon Publications, 2100 North Pacific Street, Seattle, WA 98103

Although the author and publisher have made every effort to ensure the
accuracy and completeness of information contained in this book, we assume no
responsibility for errors, inaccuracies, omissions, or any inconsistencies herein.
Any slights of people, places, or organizations are unintentional.

First edition published in 2006.
ISBN: 0-9700455-6-5
The Library of Congress Cataloging-in-Publication Data
is available from the publisher.

ATTENTION CORPORATIONS, UNIVERSITIES,
COLLEGES, AND PROFESSIONAL ORGANIZATIONS:
Quantity discounts are available on bulk purchases
of this book for educational purposes. Special books or
book excerpts can also be created to fit specific needs.
For information, please contact:
Benevon Publications
2100 North Pacific Street, Seattle, WA 98103
888-322-9357

ACKNOWLEDGEMENTS

I continue to marvel at the number of books that exist in libraries and bookstores, given the amount of work it takes to write even one. For their role in conceiving, designing, and editing this book, and for their dedication to getting our message out to the broader public, I am so grateful to our outstanding team, led by our superb senior editor Elizabeth Smith. Sincere thanks to Ann Overton, Miriam Lisco, and Paulette Eickman for their expertise and to Bobbi Nodell for her persistence. Special thanks to Stephanie Nelson, Suzanne Shoemaker, Alan Axelrod, our staff, coaches and instructors, and all of the nonprofit organizations we have the privilege of working with as we shift the conversation about fundraising from suffering and scarcity to joy and abundance.

Also by Terry Axelrod:

Raising More Money—
A Step-by-Step Guide to
Building Lifelong Donors

Raising More Money—
The Point of Entry Handbook

Raising More Money—
The Ask Event Handbook

TABLE OF CONTENTS

Shift Your Actions

PREFACE

As the mother of two children and a long-time community volunteer, I know how painful fundraising can be. Selling your daughter's share of holiday candy, raising money for your son's little league, and filling tables for school galas and auctions just seems to come with the territory of being a mom.

As the founder of three nonprofit organizations, I know firsthand the constant struggle of fundraising to survive. I saw the time and energy wasted raising quick money from one-time donors each year, but back then there was nowhere to go to learn anything more than the basics.

So in 1995, I designed the Benevon Model (formerly Raising More Money Model) of fundraising. We have trained and coached more than 2,000 organizations in the US, Canada, and Europe to implement this easy, organic system that focuses donors on the real mission of their favorite nonprofit. This model works for all kinds of organizations and programs—no matter what size your budget, your community, or your staff. In fact, it works even if you don't have a staff! All you need is a group of dedicated and enthusiastic volunteers, and you, too, can create a long-term, sustainable financial future for your favorite organization or cause.

The old reality of fundraising begins with the idea that money is scarce, so we must constantly compete, beg, and muscle our way to success. The Benevon system is built on an entirely new way of thinking about fundraising. It recognizes that resources are abundant and that individuals are looking for ways to express their caring, appreciation, and generosity by supporting worthwhile organizations and causes they truly believe in.

In this book, you will learn the basics of how to change your thinking, your focus, and your actions from the drudgery of the old reality to the joy of the new reality of fundraising. So, if you have an organization you are passionate about, and you are willing to make the shift and go to work, you can become a champion fundraiser in less than a year.

I know the joy of fundraising, and I am excited to pass that joy on to you. Not only will you be raising more money soon, you will have fun doing it!

Terry Axelrod

SHIFT YOUR
THINKING

Do you really want to keep raising money the same way you always have? Wouldn't you like to get off that treadmill of one-year-at-a-time grants, letters, and special events, with no assurance of sustained giving? This could be the year to break that cycle and build a new base of donors who understand and truly believe in your mission, donors who want to become involved in ways that are uniquely meaningful to them.

The Benevon system (formerly Raising More Money) is built on an entirely new way of thinking about fundraising. So say goodbye to the old reality of scarcity and year-to-year survival and get ready to shift your thinking into the new reality of abundance and a system for building and cultivating lifelong donors.

CHAPTER 1

FROM SCARCITY TO ABUNDANCE

The fundraising most of us know is based on a myth —the myth that there is not enough money to go around. Believing that myth creates a culture of scarcity in which nonprofit organizations feel they must compete with each other not just for funds and resources, but for their very survival.

I believe that this mindset is not necessary; in fact, it can even be an obstacle to achieving financial sustainability. The key to getting off the year-to-year fundraising treadmill and moving towards long-term sustainable funding is to shift your thinking and leave behind the myth of scarcity for a context of abundance.

Once you do that, you will see that resources can be abundant. Charitable giving in America has surpassed $250 billion per year in recent years, of which more than 80% comes from individuals, according to the annual report *Giving USA*. And, according to Claude Rosenberg of the NewTithing Group, Americans could substantially increase what they are currently giving to charity without changing their lifestyles.

Still, the myth of scarcity persists in shaping our thinking, our focus, and our actions. The Benevon Model (formerly Raising More Money Model) is based on a new reality, the reality of abundance. By following the simple ideas and actions outlined in this book, you will find yourself operating from abundance and raising more money more easily than ever.

The Old Reality of Fundraising	The Joy of Fundraising
The myth of scarcity: There is never enough money to go around.	The reality of abundance: The resources you need are in abundant supply.
You need to attract new donors each year to stay afloat, and you need to find even more new donors to grow.	Take better care of the donors you already have. They will attract others and become lifelong partners in your work.
In order to get people to give, you must entertain them and give them something first.	Donors give to causes they truly believe in.
Effective fundraisers convey the essence of their organization's work through well-documented and clearly-presented facts and statistics.	While myth-busting facts are important, effective fundraisers know donors respond best when they are moved by powerful stories of how your work affects the lives of those you serve.
All donors can be cultivated in the same way.	Each donor is a special individual who flourishes when treated with a personal touch.

Volunteers give time, not money. Don't bother trying to turn them into donors.	Volunteers and donors are motivated by the same reasons. Cultivate your volunteers with love and care and many will become lifelong donors.
Everyone knows the traits and demographics of the ideal big donors.	Today, anyone can become a major donor. Treat everyone who comes in contact with your organization as if they have that potential.
Asking for money is a difficult and tricky business. And sometimes it is downright scary.	Asking for money can be as easy and natural as picking ripened fruit—for both you and your donors.
Spend your time seeking out big, one-time gifts.	Your most committed donors want to be part of your long-term growth and financial stability.
Endowments are only for big organizations, not for smaller, lesser-known nonprofits.	Every nonprofit, regardless of size, can have a fund that covers its annual operating costs.

CHAPTER 2

THINK LIKE A DONOR

How do donors think about contributing? What motivates them not just to give money, but to become long-time financial supporters of worthy organizations and causes?

Here are the major characteristics I have discovered that are common to lifelong donors:

- They see themselves as key players and partners in your work.
- They believe passionately in your purpose and mission.
- They care deeply about the work you do and the results you achieve.

- They feel connected to the mission of the organization and its extended family of volunteers and supporters.
- Their greatest joy is knowing their giving makes a difference.

If these are the donors you want to attract to your organization, you need to see the world of giving and fundraising from their point of view. Once you are standing in their shoes, the work of fundraising will look different to you.

You will find yourself looking for ways to get the word out as widely as possible about the great work your organization is doing. You want to find those thousands of donors out there for whom your work will have special meaning. Perhaps someone in their family has needed the help you provide or your cause has always been close to their heart.

Donors who have an emotional connection to your cause will remain passionate supporters of your organization for the long term. They feel that your organization's mission and purpose are vital in our world today and in creating a better future. They care about the results of your work, and their gifts are intended to make a difference in what you can accomplish.

They will also want to be involved in your organization. For some donors that means taking an active role as a volunteer or pitching in from time to time with a big event. But for every lifelong donor, it means staying connected to and informed about the work you are doing and the results you are producing.

These donors take pride in their involvement with you, and they also are likely to become the biggest promoters of your work. For them, a gift to your animal shelter, spiritual retreat center, or child abuse program is a gift made joyfully. It is a way they express who they are, and it affirms their own hopes and dreams for the future.

By helping others discover the joy of true contribution, you will discover that fundraising itself naturally becomes a joyful and rewarding process. That is the secret of the joy of fundraising.

CHAPTER 3

ASK FROM ABUNDANCE

Most people do not like asking for money. Our society has all sorts of cultural hang-ups about money. One of the biggest is that it is simply not polite to discuss money. Add to that the cultural hang-up that it is not polite to ask for anything, and it is no wonder fund-raising is more associated with dread than with joy.

The key to easy, natural asking is two-fold:

- Ask people for what you know they have plenty of, since whatever people have in abundance is easier to share or give.

- Ask people to give when you know they are ready to be asked, which removes any feeling of guilt or manipulation from the process.

I call this asking from abundance, and with a little practice, you can become a master.

Your first job with donors and potential donors is to discover what it is they have in abundance, and then to ask them only for that. You are no longer looking for sacrificial donations. You want to know in advance that each donor can easily and naturally say yes to what you will be asking for. This is the only way people can contribute freely, rather than give out of guilt. A guilt gift is often a scarcity gift—a gift that requires the donor to sacrifice. A true contribution, on the other hand, comes from abundance.

Even if you get less than you hoped for, you will have left your donors with a positive experience of giving. That way, they will look forward to staying in contact with your organization as you deepen your relationship further before asking them to give again.

The second part of successful, terror-free asking is the answer to only one question: Is this person ready to be asked? Another way of saying it is: "Have we gotten to know this person enough so that it would feel natural to them if we ask for a financial contribution to the organization now?"

If your instincts tell you it is too early to ask someone or that it would be awkward to ask now, trust those instincts. Take the time to get to know the person better and cultivate them until they are really ready to give. By the time you ask, you should know the donor so well that asking is nothing more than nudging the inevitable.

The lifelong value of a donor is so great, you should never jeopardize that relationship. At every turn, ask the donor's permission to proceed to the next level of courtship, letting the donor at all times be the person who drives the pace and timing of the conversation. Your ultimate objective with donors is always to earn and maintain their trust and permission to ask them for whatever you truly need.

CHAPTER 4

RECOGNIZE DONORS WITH RESULTS

D onors give to your organization because they believe you are making a difference in a cause they care about. They value your work and want to support you in changing the world. Their gifts are investments in the work they expect you to accomplish.

So it follows that results are the best way to show your recognition and appreciation for your donors. Most donors don't need plaques or trinkets, which often cause donors to question your spending priorities.

Donors want to see what their gifts allowed you to accomplish—specific facts and stories of how they changed the lives of real people. This is how they will know their money was put to the best use in your programs and services.

They want to hear about the women they helped shelter from domestic violence, the lonely senior citizens whose lives are brightened by your daily visits, or the inner-city children who were inspired by their first encounter with organic gardening at your community farm. Tell your supporters, in person if you can, or through newsletters, e-mail, and phone calls, how someone's life was changed by the programs they made possible.

In addition to stories, do not underestimate the power of facts and statistics on donors. Share as much detail as you can about the progress you have made, the number of people you have expanded to reach, and the effectiveness of your work. Explain the statistics that show the impact your orchestra program has on the math scores of the children you serve, the track record of your life skills program, the number of affordable houses you have built for struggling families, or the percentage of the troubled teens who go on to graduate from college after participating in your mentoring program.

Instead of fancy baubles or plaques, find inexpensive and personal ways to thank your donors and connect them to your mission. Have the students from one of your classrooms hand deliver a scroll of paper with their handprints and thank-you messages; stop by with a rescued dog and pictures of the abused animals the donor helped rescue; or send a simple personal letter from a staff member or volunteer with a signed photo of the grateful recipients of your organization's services.

Whether yours is a complex research program, a public policy group, or a local health services clinic, there is a compelling way to recognize your donors with the facts about what their money allowed you to do and the firsthand stories about the lives it changed. By recognizing and honoring your donors this way, you will make lasting friends. This deeper recognition of the difference they make is the thanks they really want, and it will cause them to remain loyal to your organization for a lifetime and to keep asking, "How else can I help you?"

CHAPTER 5

APPRECIATE YOUR BOARD

The Golden Rule of working with your board members is to treat them as you would want to be treated. In most cases, that means being even nicer to them than you already are.

In the Benevon Model, board members are not responsible for fundraising or asking others for money. They are volunteers who are giving you the gift of their time and attention. In today's world, those gifts are more precious than money.

Treat each board member with the care and respect with which you would treat major donors. If, over time, you consistently shower them with personal attention and respect, many of them will naturally become significant donors.

Make sure you meet with each board member individually once a year so you understand what interests them most about your organization. Find out why they joined your board in the first place and what keeps them involved. Keep their specific interests foremost in your mind in every interaction with them. Let go of any expectations that their interests will ever change, but stay in close contact so that you will know if they do.

Accept the 20-60-20 rule when it comes to fundraising and your board. That is, 20% of the board will enjoy being involved in fundraising, 60% will be neutral about it, and the remaining 20% will want nothing to do with it.

For those board members who want to help with fundraising, there are three easy ways they can participate:

- Invite people to introductory events. If your board members did nothing more than this, they would still make an enormous contribution to the future of your organization. Board members can even host an introductory event of their own, perhaps focused on a particular civic, professional, or social group they belong to.

- Thank donors for gifts. Ask your board members to telephone individual donors just to thank them. Not all board members will want to do this, but once a few of them report on how wonderful the experience was at the next board meeting, others may offer to jump in.
- Give money themselves. You need to be able to tell your community that 100% of your board gives money personally to your organization, regardless of the amount.

Your board members are some of your organization's biggest treasures. They already understand and appreciate your mission. They know the need for operating funds to keep things running. And many will have no problem making five- or ten-year financial commitments to your organization.

CHAPTER 6

VOLUNTEERS ARE DONORS, TOO

What do volunteers and lifelong donors have in common? Just about everything. In fact, the characteristics of lifelong donors and volunteers are identical. As I said in chapter 2, these characteristics are:

- They see themselves as key players and partners in your work.
- They believe passionately in your purpose and mission.
- They care deeply about the work you do and the results you achieve.
- They feel connected to the organization, part of a community of volunteers and supporters.
- Their greatest joy is knowing they make a difference.

Of course, when you think about it, giving time is a lot like giving money. Volunteers and donors are all seeking meaningful ways to contribute to your cause, and they are all providing valuable resources for your organization.

According to *Giving and Volunteering in the United States*, 56% of American adults volunteer. This is an increase of nearly 14% in two years. Clearly, volunteering is no longer just for the wealthy or retired. Volunteers, like donors, are looking for the chance to make a difference in something they care about. More and more of us are turning to volunteer work to round out our lives.

Volunteers, like donors, respond best when they can see the impact of their efforts. Volunteers want to know their contribution is effective and changing lives. This is what deepens their involvement and commitment to your organization and its mission.

Shift your perspective about volunteers from one that is organization-centered to one that is volunteer-centered. Allow your volunteers to design their own roles and job descriptions based on their personal interests. Some will want you to have ideas for them; others will know right away what they want to do. In any case, they will appreciate a customized approach with personal attention to their preferences. They will know you are listening to them, nurturing them, and acknowledging them when they see the impact their contribution makes.

Satisfied volunteers are also among your best ambassadors at spreading the word about your good work. When friends or acquaintances ask them what they have been doing lately, their work with your organization is likely to figure prominently in their conversation. And with enough cultivation and involvement, many of your volunteers will choose to become financial donors to your organization. According to *Giving and Volunteering in the United States*, 90% of volunteers also give money. Conversely, many of your financial donors may also want to get involved as volunteers.

Create the opportunity for your volunteers to contribute their talent and time on their own terms, and you will be continually surprised at the unexpected range of resources they provide.

CHAPTER 7

PLANT THE SEEDS OF SUSTAINABILITY

T he real work of fundraising is providing a future of ongoing stability for your organization. In a world of abundance, sustainable funding is possible—and necessary—for every nonprofit.

A fundraising plan focused on financial sustainability will ultimately take the suffering out of funding basic operational needs and allow your organization to focus on its mission—be it curing a disease, cleaning up the environment, or improving the lives of migrant workers.

The first step to sustainable funding is having the courage to think it is possible.

As impossible and out of reach as sustainable funding may seem, it has to start somewhere. A few years ago, I interviewed twelve organizations of all sizes that had significant endowment funds. These are organizations that still run active, donor-centered fundraising programs, involving new people. They are not the kind of organizations you would expect to have solid endowments.

In every case, they acknowledged the foresight and vision of someone who had come before them and said, "Enough is enough! We've got a great organization here, doing great work. We need to leave it knowing that the people in charge can focus on fulfilling the mission and not worry each year about the next fundraising scheme to bail them out."

Eventually, they also asked: "How much money would it take to endow the operational funding gap here? How much would it really cost to achieve sustainability for this organization?" They didn't back away when they saw the size of the number. They began working systematically to fund an endowment. They never lost sight of their goal: financial self-sustainability.

The next step toward sustainable funding is to clarify what that means to your organization. For some it may come in the form of a large cash reserve or rainy day account, for others it may be earned income or a social-purpose business venture. For most groups, though, the key to long-term financial sustainability is an endowment fund that generates enough return on investment to meet or exceed the basic operating cash you need to raise each year.

The Benevon Model is about creating a system that reliably generates more and more happy donors who give money to your organization. As you take care of these donors, they will bring in others who want be involved. Over time, the circle of people supporting your organization will grow, and you will have an increasing number of loyal donors who have chosen to make a multiple-year financial commitment.

Sustainable funding for the mission of each nonprofit organization is possible, even for the smallest of groups, if they have a clearly defined goal and a systematic approach maintained over time. You could be the person with the courage and vision to spearhead the sustainable funding effort for your organization. Sustainable funding is within your reach!

SHIFT YOUR
FOCUS

*The old reality of fundraising focused on a year-to year strug-
gle with targets, grant proposals, and chasing after every possible source of funding. It often felt like hand-to-hand combat,
and even more often led to a hand-to-mouth existence. The
focus was on immediate needs, and there was very little time
to think of the future or plan for the long term.*

*As you shift your thinking to this abundance-based model
of fundraising, you will find that your focus shifts, too. Instead
of concentrating on day-to-day needs, your attention shifts to
nurturing the passion for your organization's work, to devel-
oping the most effective way to communicate about that work,
and to the care and cultivation of your donors and potential
donors.*

CHAPTER 8

LOOK FOR HIDDEN TREASURE

Every nonprofit organization has a wealth of hidden treasure just waiting to be uncovered. To find it, you only need to ask the people who already know and love your organization's mission and work. In a perfectly organic way, these people can easily lead you to others who also will become passionate about your work.

Here are nine easy steps to finding new supporters using a simple exercise called the Treasure Map:

1. Gather a team of people who know and love your organization's work. The more diverse your team, the better your Treasure Map will be.

2. Get out a large piece of paper and colored markers. Draw a small circle in the center of the page and put the name of your organization in the circle.

3. Surround your organization, like the spokes on a wheel, with all the other groups you come in contact with on a regular basis. Start with groups like your board, staff, volunteers, donors, vendors, and other groups in the community you interact with regularly. You may be able to subdivide some groups like your board into former board, former board presidents, founding board members, etc.

4. With a marker of a second color, list the resources each of these groups has in abundance. Why? Because it is much easier to give away something that you already have plenty of. For example, your board in general might have an abundance of passion, commitment, expertise, contacts, and money. Your volunteers may have time or extra household items you need.

5. Ask yourselves what would be the self-interest of each of these groups in learning more about your cause. Examples include: to learn new skills, to please the boss, to get a paycheck (for staff), to

socialize, to polish their image in the community, or simply to feel good about making a difference. There will probably be a wide range of reasons for learning more and becoming involved with your organization, and they are all perfectly valid motivations. Write those reasons in a marker of a new color next to each group.

6. Now, add in some fantasy categories. Who is not yet on your map that you would love to have associated with your organization? Is there a certain category (like the media) or a certain individual (like a well-respected business leader or clergy member) whose involvement would contribute a whole world of support and credibility?

7. Next, draw connecting lines between those groups on your Treasure Map that already talk to each other. If your board and vendors talk only occasionally, you might draw a dotted line. For those groups who don't talk to each other at all, draw no connecting lines. Be sure to include your fantasy groups. Who on your Treasure Map might already be talking with them?

8. Stand back from your Treasure Map and notice which groups have the most lines connecting them to other groups. These groups are the key to involving others.

9. Make a list of at least thirty people from those key groups who would naturally want to learn more about your group. Then begin to cultivate, involve, and inspire this group of people first. If you do a good job, they will start talking about your organization to the other groups they are connected to on the Treasure Map and even begin involving them for you.

CHAPTER 9

NURTURE
YOUR PASSION

Your passion for the work of your organization inspires others. So one of the most important jobs of every fundraiser is keeping your own passion alive.

There are two reliable ways to stay in touch with whatever it is about the organization's mission that moves and inspires you.

The first is to ask yourself why you got involved and why you have stayed involved. What is the real reason this organization is important to you? Be honest with yourself and write down your answers.

Better yet, do this exercise with a small group of staff and volunteers. It is a great way to begin a retreat or informal group meeting and is much more powerful than socializing. As people sit down to begin the formal part of the meeting or retreat, ask them to introduce themselves and to say why they got involved with the organization in the first place and why they have stayed involved.

Some of the stories may be very personal and moving, others may be amusing. But as the stories spill out, members of the group will rediscover their connection to the organization. At the same time, they will gain a deeper respect for and connection to each other. People will come to appreciate—and be more tolerant of—the quirky or challenging members of the group.

In the end, all who participate in this exercise will have new energy and enthusiasm for telling the story of the organization to the community. They will be reminded of just how important the work of this organization is and why they want to help out.

The second way to nurture your passion is to leave the office and the telephones and go out where the work of your organization is taking place. If you are involved at a school, visit the classrooms and spend time with the students. If you are involved at an animal shelter, spend some time with the animals. Immerse yourself, even if only for an hour or two, in the real world of what your organization does. You are sure to return to your desk with a new sense of passion and urgency about the work to be done.

CHAPTER 10

FIND YOUR ESSENTIAL STORY

E very nonprofit organization has an "Essential Story"—one that conveys the emotional essence of your work powerfully and memorably each time it is told. Long after people forget specific facts, they should remember this story.

Your organization's Essential Story may be a true story about one particular person or family, or it may be a composite of several stories of real people whose lives have been changed by your organization. There is always a way to relate your mission to the changed life of one individual or family, even if you're dealing with an abstract policy issue.

The Essential Story has the power to move people emotionally and to call them to action. Indeed, you will know you have crafted your Essential Story when it moves you every time you tell it. This emotional connection is what creates the deeper, lasting relationships that lead to long-term giving and support.

Begin writing your Essential Story by investigating what it is about your cause that engages people. What calls them to become involved and stay involved? For a camp or college, that emotional connection may be a longing for the past. For an environmental group, it may be a dream of leaving our children a healthy planet.

Gather a small group together and discuss the following questions:

- What originally moved you about the mission of the organization? Why did you decide to get involved in the first place? Share your stories and watch for common threads.
- What cherished cultural values and ideals does your organization deal with?
- Why do others say they want to be involved with your organization? What moves them to give their time or money?

Once you find the emotional connection, you can incorporate it into every communication through an Essential Story about how your work impacts people's lives.

This Essential Story has three distinct stages:

STAGE 1: THE "BEFORE" STAGE
Choose one person's story, give the person a fictitious name, and briefly describe in vivid language their situation before they came in contact with your group.

STAGE 2: THE "INTERVENTION"
What specific services or support did they receive from you? What was your personal observation of them at that time?

STAGE 3: THE "AFTER" STAGE
What are the results of the intervention? How has life changed for this person? What is now possible for them? What does this person now say about his or her life? How are they giving back to others?

Write out the Essential Story and have a team of people from your organization practice telling it. Work on refining the story until you can tell it in two minutes or less and everyone in the group feels the emotional impact.

Once you have mastered your first Essential Story, create other versions of your Essential Story you can tell when you introduce people to your work. This will give you a dependable way for anyone in your organization to successfully convey the emotional essence of your work and form the emotional connections with potential donors that inspire long-term giving.

CHAPTER 11

SIMPLIFY AND DEMYSTIFY

Inspiration and emotion are never enough to carry the day. Potential donors also need information and hard facts about your organization's work.

But too much information about your various programs or too many complicated facts can overwhelm people. A few memorable, surprising facts and a brief description of a few of your programs is plenty. You want to pique people's interest and leave them with a basic understanding of what you do.

Instead of trying to cover everything, make your motto "simplify and demystify" when you explain your work to new people.

First, select three of your organization's programs or areas of work to highlight. There is no need to list all your programs and services; choose the three programs or services that will give people a general sense of the breadth of your work. Later on in the relationship, when you know the person better, you can connect them with the particular program that best matches their interests.

Next, find three facts that will dispel the myths and misconceptions about your cause or the people you serve. Usually these facts also answer some of the questions you are frequently asked. This is your opportunity to high-light little-known information about your work.

For example, a group serving street youth knew that people's stereotypes of lazy, drug-addicted, dangerous kids could be dispelled by statistics about the numbers of street youth who had been abused by their family mem-bers and considered life on the streets safer than life at home.

You can also use these facts to convey the need for your services and the effectiveness of your work. If you're raising money for a school band, show the value of your work with statistics correlating music education and aca-demic success.

Although these facts are simple, they will evoke powerful emotions. A sexual assault center developed these three moving facts:

- There are sixty cases of sexual assault reported every day right here in our community. Of those, we are able to serve only five new clients per day. We have to turn away the others who request services.
- Last year, we served approximately 1,200 women, men, and children here in our community.
- Last year, our oldest client was eighty-six and our youngest was nine months old.

When you keep it simple and use facts that demystify your work, people are left with a more powerful understanding of what you do and why your work is important.

CHAPTER 12

CREATE A SENSE OF URGENCY

Potential donors want to know your organization needs them. They want to know their gift will make a big difference in what you are able to do. They want you to convey not just the excellent work you are already doing, but also the lives that still urgently need your help.

In other words, people are more likely to give when they understand the urgency of your work.

The most effective way to do this is to show them the gap between where you are now and where you could be if only you had more resources—which is where they come in. They can help you to reach more people in need or better support the people you are serving now.

Portray the gap for them—not in minute detail, but broadly enough so there is room for people to fill in the blanks or expand around the edges—to add what they alone can uniquely contribute.

Here are some examples of how to convey the urgency of your work:

- Show people one simple pie chart about your budget, income sources, trends, etc.
- Share some of the key strategic issues you are facing right now—how to grow your highly successful programs, develop a scholarship fund, or expand your travel fund to support future debate teams to compete nationally.
- Suggest several programs you would like to start or expand, based on specific examples of people you've had to turn away.
- Mention in-kind goods and services you need.
- Mention capital needs you might have. What more could you do if you had that new building, new van, or new roof?
- Even if you're in a gorgeous new building, explain that it happened thanks to many generous donors and tell them what else you still need.

- Tell them a story about the lives you still want to change.
- Make a wish list (without dollar amounts; you're not asking for money yet) with a range of items, from old sneakers to a new gymnasium.

People want to hear about your organization's real day-to-day frustrations as well as your successes. They want to know about the kinds of requests you have to turn down and the people you have to turn away. This will show them how they can fit in and help you expand your valuable work so you can do even more.

CHAPTER 13

SHOWCASE YOUR VISIONARY LEADER

Every nonprofit organization has a "Visionary Leader." For most organizations, it is your executive director or your most senior staff member. If you have no staff, it is your board chair or top-ranking volunteer leader.

(Note: If you are trying to raise money and lead the organization by yourself, then the Visionary Leader is you! Resist the temptation of deferring to someone who sounds more polished or choosing a well-recognized figurehead from the community. It is your passion and ownership that will make the difference.)

When people attend your events, they expect to hear from the Visionary Leader. Potential donors want to know there is someone in charge with a solid vision for the organization's future and the determination to achieve it.

Most Visionary Leaders are very passionate people, yet when asked to speak about their organizations, they often default to a dry speech about the organization's programs, services, and challenges.

In contrast, the sole purpose of this special talk is to inspire people about the urgent nature of the mission. The Visionary Leader's true passion and emotion about the organization's work must come through. After all, this is the person in charge. Who else would we look to for vision and inspiration?

The Visionary Leader talk lasts for just five to seven minutes, and it includes the following elements:

- Begin with a short personal story about how the leader got involved and why the leader has stayed with the organization. Your Visionary Leader must be willing to tell their own story, open up, and show emotion and passion.

- Give a very brief outline of the mission and history of the organization. When was the organization founded, and by whom? Why does it really exist? What values does it teach, encourage, or represent? How has it evolved and grown over time?
- Explain the gap between where the organization is now and where it needs to go to fulfill the next phase of its mission. Identify the number of people who are unserved or underserved now. How many people do you have to turn away? How does the absence of those needed programs and services in the community impact the people listening to this talk?
- Convey the vision for the future of the organization and what it will take to fulfill the mission. Where does the leader want to be five to ten years from now? Cite examples of the additional programs that could be offered and additional people who could be served.
- Wrap up the talk by explaining the impact the broader community would feel if the organization were to accomplish these goals.

This Visionary Leader talk is a powerful tool that can be used again and again at your events to connect people to your work. It is well worth taking the time to craft it carefully and to coach your Visionary Leader to deliver it brilliantly. Paint the picture, and excite the community with your leader's vision!

CHAPTER 14

GET PERSONAL

Y our donors and potential donors will notice and appreciate it when you customize your contacts with them according to their interests and needs. This shows them they are important to you. It makes make them feel special and connected to the organization, and it will certainly have an impact on the gifts they eventually make.

In the Benevon Model, there are four main ways to customize your contacts:

- Make it personal with one-on-one contacts that allow for a dialog. These may be face-to-face, telephone, or e-mail contacts. Show the person that you are speaking only to them, and give them an easy way to respond, ask questions, and give advice. Above all, show that you are listening to them, using their advice, and remembering what they said.

- Keep your contacts relevant to each donor's interests. Your donors will be most responsive and enthusiastic when the contacts you have with them match their unique interests and needs. For example, a potential donor to a disease-related research organization might enjoy a special lunch meeting with a research scientist or staff member in charge of a project of keen interest to the donor.

- Time your contacts to the donor's pace. In the beginning, before you know them well, follow up in a three- to five-day timeframe. You want to follow up while their most recent contact with you is still fresh in their minds. Then adjust your timing once you learn their preference.

- Contact the donor through the medium they prefer. Until you find out what that is, you may want to vary the medium through which you communicate. You can dash off a quick e-mail to let them know the status of a request or leave a brief voice-mail message inviting them to a related event to keep your cause in their mind. An occasional hand-written letter from you or a recipient of your services, a photograph, or a hand-made work of art (from a child, for example) can arrive by mail. Of course, there is no substitute for the in-person meeting. The more you get to know people, the more you can tailor your interactions to their preferred medium and style.

You also can incorporate these four criteria into many of the contacts you already have with donors. For example, many organizations use a newsletter to inform people about their work. It is generally sent by bulk mail with an address label. To make a donor feel more special, you could put a handwritten note on it, put it in a first-class envelope, or fax it directly. If the newsletter is sent by e-mail, a personal salutation is effective. Give your subscribers a way to contact you personally with feedback or to change their contact information.

If you wanted to make that same newsletter even more personal, you could call or e-mail the person in advance to tell them it is coming and let them know there is an article about the project or person they are most interested in. You can invite their response or reaction. You or someone from your board can even call and tell them you would like to meet to show them the article personally.

Begin the process of getting personal by choosing just a few potential donors who have expressed real interest in your work. It takes only a little more time to personalize your contacts this way, and the results will be immediate. You will be working smarter, not harder.

CHAPTER 15

FOCUS ON THE LONG TERM

I n the Benevon Model, a critical part of building a system of lifelong donors is a Multiple-Year Giving Society.

A Multiple-Year Giving Society is a group of higher-level donors who pledge to give an unrestricted gift of at least $1,000 a year for five years. This society has a special name, and members get special recognition from your organization.

Many groups are reluctant to launch a Multiple-Year Giving Society, saying, "Our donors would never go for that." In truth, what they often mean is they would feel uncomfortable asking for multiple-year pledges.

But asking for multiple-year contributions is not for the organization; it is for the donor. Multiple-Year Donors are people who already love you and in many cases have been giving to you, year after year, with relatively little contact or cultivation.

Now you are giving them an opportunity to come forward and declare themselves part of your organizational family. Some will say, "No, thank you." Others will ask, "What took you so long to notice?"

Start your Multiple-Year Giving Society with pledges of five years. Organizations bold enough to write those few extra words, "for five years," on their pledge cards almost always wish they had done it sooner.

Since your Multiple-Year Giving Society will be around for years, take the time to name it carefully. For your overall society, consider the name of a famous person who has championed your cause, or perhaps the name of one of your founders. Or you can choose a name that has a direct connection to the essence of your work, like the Full Plate Society for a food bank or the Hope for Children Society for a children's home.

You should aim at having only three levels of giving in your Multiple-Year Giving Society. These levels are called Units of Service, and they are either:

- $1,000, $5,000, and $10,000 a year for each of the next five years *or*
- $1,000, $10,000, and $25,000 a year for each of the next five years

Choose your levels based on the largest gift your organization received in the last two years. If it was $10,000 or more, then you belong at the three higher levels. If it was under $10,000, use the three lower levels.

The names of your levels are intended to personalize your work and give donors a sense of what their gifts can do. Donors also like to see that the three levels relate logically to one another.

Think through your options carefully to come up with units that capture the essence of what your donors are giving to. For example, if the lowest level is "sponsor a child," your middle level could be "sponsor a family," and your highest level "sponsor a neighborhood" or a community. Be sure to explain to your donors that these are really unrestricted gifts and that these levels are just an example of what their money can do.

Of course, these levels won't be a good fit for everyone, which is why you'll always have a space on your pledge card for people to write in their own gift amount and length of pledge, as well as a box they can check to indicate that they have advice or other forms of support for you.

This process gives your donors guidance without pressure, and your fill-in-the-blank option gives them the freedom to give at whatever level they are comfortable. Multiple-year asking, if done consistently and with cultivation, will get your organization off the yearly treadmill and build the lifelong donors you are looking for.

SHIFT YOUR
ACTIONS

Once your thinking and focus shift to the new reality of abundance-based fundraising, your actions will easily follow. Every event, meeting, or one-on-one conversation will become an opportunity to connect with friends and donors. You will recognize that you have no right to expect a true contribution from someone who has not been informed, inspired, listened to, and involved. You will let the donor determine the timing and pace of the relationship, ever vigilant of the donor's readiness to give again.

In adopting this mission-based fundraising approach, you don't have to shift everything at once. You can start by setting your sights on one area, program, or event you now offer. Wherever you begin, you will find that you naturally establish, one donor at a time, a base of lifelong supporters who are delighted to be part of your organizational family.

CHAPTER 16

BUILD A TEAM

It takes a team of committed individuals to shift the thinking and actions of an organization in a lasting way. In other words, you can not do this alone!

No matter how small your organization, there are at least a few other people who care about making your organization financially sustainable. Consider engaging these people as your team as you shift your fundraising from a context of scarcity to one of abundance.

The first step in building a team is selecting a team leader. This may be an obvious choice. For example, if you are beginning this process yourself, you are probably the team leader by default! If you have a few people already willing to join your team, you will need to decide as a group which of you will be the team leader.

The team leader's responsibilities include:

- Coordinating and implementing your organization's annual fundraising plan.
- Managing the team to meet deadlines and complete assigned tasks.
- Ensuring that all data is captured in the database tracking system.
- Personally taking on or delegating all tasks needed to fulfill each element of the fundraising plan.

Who else to include on your team? Look for people you enjoy working with who are:

- Dedicated to your organization's work.
- Passionate about your cause.
- Willing and able to serve on the team for one year.
- Dependable, with a solid track record of following through on what they say they will do.
- Good communicators.

The specific responsibilities of each team member will vary depending on that person's interests and strengths. As a whole, the responsibilities of team members include:

- Organizing, attending, and inviting people to events.
- Making follow-up and thank-you calls.
- Cultivating new supporters and existing donors.
- Asking people for money, when appropriate.

The ideal team generally has a total of seven people: two staff members (or volunteers if you have no staff), two board members, and three volunteers. Keep in mind that this is an ideal scenario, and your team's composition may vary. It is far more important to find people with the qualities you are looking for than to try to fit your team to these criteria.

If you don't have seven people right away, you can begin with a few committed people and expand your team as you connect with new people who are passionate about your mission. It is much better to wait for the right people than to fill your team with people who aren't really a good fit.

Passionate, dependable team members are the people who will get your organization off the annual fundraising treadmill and onto the path toward sustainable funding.

CHAPTER 17

TRACK RELATIONSHIPS

Most people are much quicker to acknowledge the importance of a good data-tracking system than they are to volunteer to organize it. Although it may not be the most exciting or glamorous part of fundraising, a centralized tracking system is an invaluable and lasting legacy for your organization.

There are many good tracking systems to choose from, including Web-based systems as well as more traditional desktop software systems. You will want a data-tracking system that meets the following criteria:

- It tracks relationships and contacts over time, in addition to contact information and gift history.

- It is easy for everyone on your team to record notes about every single contact with a donor. (The only exception to this is the financial data, which needs to be entered by one or two well-trained people and remain confidential.)
- It interfaces well with your Web site. This will allow the information from forms, surveys, event registrations, and e-commerce—including donations—to be captured directly into the database.
- It delivers and stores both individual and mass e-mail.
- It integrates with your calendar and reminder system.

To determine what to track, look first at what you are already tracking. You probably have lists of current donors, volunteers, board members, past board members, staff, and former staff. If you already are a diligent tracker, you may have other information, like which events people have attended, which mailings they have responded to, and who introduced them to the organization.

You will find there is data to enter for every event and contact your organization has. For example, you will want to know how each person in your database was referred to your organization. For follow-up calls, note the date you called, any messages left before you reached them, and what they said on the call. Create separate records for the new people they suggest you call.

For your fundraising events, track whether a guest RSVP'd, the amount of the donor's gift or pledge on the day of the event, and the dates these pledges were paid off or increased (perhaps at subsequent events).

It is also important to track when and how each donor was thanked. Makes notes of any other feedback they have given you since the event. Decide on the next contact you will have with them, and tie that to your "to-do" list and calendar for that date.

While it may seem a daunting task, once it is up and running, a good system makes the data-tracking process easy and painless. You and your team will spend less time in front of the computer and more time personally cultivating donors and potential donors.

CHAPTER 18

START SPREADING
THE WORD

Where do you begin to spread the word to those who have never heard about your organization's great work?

A short, introductory event that educates and inspires guests is the most effective way to increase your organization's visibility in the community. These events are what will compel people to tell others about your work. They will also bring you wonderful volunteers and in-kind donations of goods and services.

An introduction to your organization can take many forms. It may be the traditional tour of your offices or clinic, a dessert gathering in someone's home, a meeting in a board member's office, a church basement, or a restaurant.

There are three key ingredients to every introductory event:

- Emotion, conveyed through touching stories of people whose lives were changed by your organization's work. You can weave in these stories with an inspirational talk from your organization's leader, a tour, live testimonials, audiotape, and letters.

- Some basic facts about your work that dispel the myths or stereotypes about what you do or the people you serve. A short overview of your top three programs and three surprising facts about your work will accomplish this.

- Capturing the names of your guests with their permission by using simple sign-in cards so you can follow up with them later.

I call these introductions Point of Entry Events, but you should give your introductory events a warm and inviting name like "Hope Tours," "Welcome Waggins" (for an animal shelter), or "Backstage Tours."

Plan to hold these one-hour events at least once a month and aim to have ten to fifteen people attend each event.

Personal, word-of-mouth invitations from a friend are by far the most effective way to invite guests to these events. This method also ensures that the inviter can prepare the guests properly by conveying the following:

- This is only a "get acquainted" introductory session.
- You will not be asked for money .
- The organization will want to hear your feedback after the event.

Since most people will attend this event only once, it is crucial that it be memorable, not merely interesting. Your goal should be to have your guests want to invite and involve future guests, which they will do only if you have truly moved and inspired them.

Once these events get going, your group's name will be well-known in the community. You won't be the "best-kept secret" anymore!

CHAPTER 19

TALKING ONE-ON-ONE

D on't wait for introductory or special events. Seize the moment and talk about your organization every chance you get.

Every one-on-one conversation is an opportunity to introduce people to your organization's work. You can do this with someone sitting next to you on a bus or plane, at a party, over the telephone, in your office or theirs.

To do this effectively, you need to create an inspiring talk that takes no more than two minutes to deliver from start to finish. These are sometimes called 'elevator speeches' because you should be able to deliver the talk in the time it takes to ride in an elevator with someone.

Be sure your talk covers these six points:

- The name of your organization.
- Your two or three favorite programs that show the breadth of your work.
- One little-known but easy to remember fact about your work.
- Why you truly love the work of the organization.
- Your favorite story about how the work of your organization changes lives.
- How to stay in contact with the person—but only if they say they are interested in learning more.

Now practice, practice, practice. Begin by having these conversations with people from your organization and with your family and friends—people you know and trust. Ask them for feedback to make sure your talk is short, jargon free, and that your passion and emotion come across. When you can do all this in two minutes, you are ready to take your talk on the road and teach others on your team to create their own two-minute talks.

Soon, the word about your organization's valuable work will be spreading around the community on its own!

CHAPTER 20

MISSIONIZE YOUR SPECIAL EVENTS

What about those events your organization already puts on every year? The auction, the gala, the walk-a-thon, the golf tournament—you may have quite a list.

It is time to transform the existing events you want to keep so they more effectively spread the word about your organization. By inserting a simple ten-minute program that conveys the essence of your work to your guests, you can easily incorporate your mission into almost any event.

In the case of a fundraising event—an auction, golf tournament, gala, concert or picnic, for example—there will be a time when people gather and, ideally, sit down. This is the time to insert that short program element. You need to have your guests' undivided attention.

Start this mission element by telling your guests: "We would not be doing our job if we didn't take advantage of having you all here today to take a few minutes to tell you about the wonderful work of our organization."

The main intention of this short program is to convey the emotional impact of your work through a powerful story, with a few surprising facts and basic information about your programs. You want to inspire people about the value and urgency of your work. You want guests at every event you host to leave knowing your organization's name and enough information about your work that they could tell a friend what your group does.

Your ten-minute program should include:

- A seven-minute talk from your organization's leader or a seven-minute emotion-packed video.
- A three-minute live testimonial from someone whose life has been touched by your work.

To wrap up this short mission element, have the emcee say, "We know most of you came today to have a nice social event (golf tournament, etc.). Perhaps now you find yourself more interested in our work. Maybe you'd even like to come to our office and visit us in person. If so, please leave us your name (fill out a card, tell your table host) so we can be in contact with you."

You can use this strategy to transform ongoing program-related events so they broadcast the news about your mission and work.

A good example is the program some Habitat for Humanity affiliates include during lunch on their Saturday "build days." As volunteers sit outside eating, the organization's leader stands up and gives a short, inspirational talk about Habitat's work. One of the people who is working on the house alongside the volunteers then gives a powerful testimonial and thanks the volunteers for helping to build this home for their family. Finally, the leader or board chair points out the person who will be calling the volunteers in the next week to get their feedback about the work day and to see if they have any further interest in learning about the organization.

As you scan your list of existing events, you'll start to see equally natural and easy ways to incorporate your mission into all the events your organization puts on each year.

CHAPTER 21

FOLLOW UP, LISTEN, AND INVOLVE

Following up your introductory events with potential donors is critical to successful fundraising. Their feedback will help you to improve the way you tell your organization's story to new people, and it may lead to further involvement for this particular person.

In the Benevon Model, there are two rules for your introductory events that make following up easy and fun:

- Always get permission to contact the person later for their feedback about what they learned.
- Make sure they know they will not be asked for money during either the introductory event or the follow-up conversation.

After the introductory event, wait a few days and then make the follow-up call. Follow up is best done in an actual voice-to-voice conversation (rather than a thank-you note or e-mail) that has the true give-and-take that can lead to further involvement.

If people don't respond after a couple of friendly voicemail messages, it is time to "bless and release" them. In other words, if they are not interested in continued contact with your organization, let them go.

The follow-up call consists of five easy steps:

1. Thank the person for coming to the event.
2. Ask them, "What did you think?"
3. Listen. This is where you will learn what you really want to know—What was it that most piqued this person's interest? If your group is working to cure a disease that has several strains to it, a woman may tell you she is most interested in the particular strain of the disease her mother now suffers from. That is a very big cue—one that will steer your future conversations. In the future, there is no need to discuss the other strains of the disease. Just focus on the one she is most concerned with. You wouldn't know how to involve her if you didn't listen closely for such cues during the follow-up call.

4. When you are sure the person is done telling you what they think, ask them, "Is there any way you could see yourself becoming involved with us?" This is not a volunteer recruitment call. It is an open-ended follow-up call, so you need to be open to whatever they suggest. And be prepared for the question they may ask in return: "What do you need?" The best answer is: "We need help spreading the word about our work by hosting or inviting people to introductory events to learn about our organization."

5. Finally, ask them, "Is there anyone else you can think of who should hear about our work?" If their contact with your organization was moving and inspiring, people will be quick to refer others. If you find that people are reluctant to refer their friends, it is likely that your event is just so-so, not stellar. After all, would you refer a good friend to something that was just so-so?

There will be some people who prefer not to get involved with your organization. The Benevon Model is designed to help you sort out the people who are "just interested" from those who have the potential to become lifelong supporters. Again, "bless and release" those who aren't interested by thanking them for their time. By letting them go without pressure, you will gain their respect and make a friend for your organization. You also will free yourself to focus your efforts on those who are passionate about your cause and want further involvement.

CHAPTER 22

GET TO KNOW
YOUR DONORS

I f your organization is like most nonprofits, you already have a list of members, subscribers, donors, or former donors you don't know personally. These people are on your lists for a reason; they have had some sort of connection to or interest in your organization. Many of them would be interested in further involvement if you took the time to get to know them and cultivate them individually.

Create a list of the people you want to get to know, and assemble a team of callers who are closely tied to your organization. The callers can do the phoning in a group one afternoon or evening, or they can make the calls on their own from their home or workplace. Tell them to take detailed notes and turn them in after the calls, since this is valuable information you will put into your tracking system to help you determine future contacts with these people.

These calls are simply meant to thank those on the list for their gift or involvement and to let them know how much you appreciate their support. Make it clear to your callers that this is NOT an opportunity to ask for contributions!

Here is a suggested outline for the call:

Hello, Ms. _____. My name is _____. I'm on the board of the _____ organization. You've been a loyal supporter for several/many years, and we're calling to thank you. (Pause for response.) Do you have a few minutes now for me to ask for your thoughts and advice?

Suggested questions:

- How did you come to know about us or become involved with us?
- What do you like about being a friend/supporter of our organization?
- What advice do you have for us?
- What could we be doing to involve more people?

To encourage further involvement with your organization, at the end of the call you can invite each person to an introductory event. Let them know they are welcome to bring others. If they agree to attend, follow up with a confirmation card and a call to reconfirm on the day before the event.

Some of the people you call will be more eager than others to increase their involvement with your organization. Some will be perfectly satisfied with their current level of involvement. You can simply thank them for their support and move on. There is no need to pressure people who aren't truly interested; you are bound to come across others who do want to learn more or get involved in some way.

CHAPTER 23

HOST AN
ASK EVENT

P eople who care about your organization's mission don't need fancy entertainment events like auctions, galas, or poker tournaments to convince them to give money. All they need is a simple, straightforward event that inspires them about the value and urgency of your work.

Benevon has created a fool-proof, mission-based fundraising event called a "Free One-Hour Ask Event." What makes this Ask Event unique?

- Guests are invited personally by someone they know.
- The event is always a free breakfast or lunch.

- It is only one hour long from beginning to end.
- Many of the guests already know and care about the organization, having attended introductory events and perhaps grown even more involved.
- The focus is on educating and inspiring, not entertaining.
- There is no pressure or expectation to give. Guests have the freedom to give as much or little as they wish.
- The event honors all donors and supporters regardless of their giving level.

Two elements of the Free One-Hour Ask Event make it particularly successful.

First, all the invitations are issued by a team of Table Captains, each of whom is responsible for filling a table with ten people at the event. Table Captains must have a passion for your organization and the ability to actually fill their table with ten people on the day of the event. Their guests are invited personally, word-of-mouth. No fancy printed invitations are needed.

Second, the program includes the following:

- An inspirational five-minute talk from your organization's leader, with a moving personal story and a brief overview of the past, present, and future goals of the organization. Emphasize why this cause is unique and why it needs support.

- A seven-minute video packed with enough emotion to touch the heart and bring your guests to tears three times. The whole purpose of this video is to show how your work impacts real people.
- A live testimonial from someone whose life was changed by your organization's work.
- The pitch, where a respected and trusted person walks guests through the pledge card. This person gives guests the option of joining a Multiple-Year Giving Society or giving whatever amount is comfortable for them.

Guests at this type of Ask Event appreciate the straightforward approach and leave the event inspired to tell others about your work. If you have the commitment and team to take on hosting a Free One-Hour Ask Event, you will find it increases your visibility and good will in the community in addition to generating exceptional financial results.

CHAPTER 24

GET READY,
GET SET...

I n addition to hosting a powerful Ask Event, there will always be times when asking someone individually is more appropriate. We call this the one-on-one Ask.

In this permission-based approach, the key to successful, terror-free one-on-one asking is the answer to only one question: Is this person ready to be asked? Have we gotten to know this person well enough that it feels natural to ask them to make a financial contribution to the organization now?

Tune into your instincts for those readiness clues, like people coming to your events, returning your calls and e-mails, asking for more information, offering advice, referring others, volunteering, and—my personal favorite—they start talking about "we."

You should be able to answer all of the following pre-Ask questions about each donor. And if you can't, that's a sign that you need to meet again and continue to cultivate this donor—by talking about and involving them in the parts of your work that most interest them—until they are sufficiently engaged.

- Exactly who will you ask? Have you cultivated all the key decision-makers? Should spouses, partners, children, parents, or business partners be included?
- Who will do the asking? Would another board member enhance the asking team? Who would this donor want to say yes to?
- Where will the Ask take place?
- Exactly what will be asked for?
- What makes you think this person is ready to be asked now? Have there been any recent cues? Put yourself in the donor's shoes. Will they feel comfortable and receptive to an Ask now?
- What are your biggest concerns, fears, and reasons for procrastinating in making this Ask? Often these are legitimate, especially if they concern donor-readiness.

- Does the person have an abundance of what you are asking for?
- What is the person's self-interest in saying yes? How good would they feel saying yes? How sorry will they feel saying no?
- What might strengthen this Ask? What could you add that would encourage this person to say yes? A memorial gift? A challenge or matching gift? More years to spread out the payment? A particular type of recognition?
- What would be possible for your organization if the person says yes?

Now, find someone to role play the Ask with you. Give them the background on the person to be asked. Tell them some of your biggest fears so they can be sure to play on them during the practice session. Then find another partner and practice again!

ASK, NATURALLY!

When you have finished your preparation and are confident that both you and your potential donor are ready, call and ask if you can meet with them face-to-face. You may want to bring along someone else from your organization who they know and respect; perhaps the executive director or board chair. Meet wherever the donor is most comfortable. This could be at your office, their office, their home, or a restaurant.

Here are some tips to help you during your Asks:

- Your agenda is to see how related and connected you can become in those few minutes you will be together. It is all about listening for every cue and being much more focused on what they are saying right now than on what you should say next.

- Know what you want to ask for in advance, and be ready to negotiate. The easiest thing is to invite them to join your existing society of donors who make multiple-year pledges at specific giving levels.
- Explain the difference that this gift would make to your organization and the impact it will have on the people you serve. You will know this donor well enough by now that you can talk about the aspects of your program that are most important to them—the after-school program, the adoption program, the chapel. Just have a natural conversation with them as if you were talking to a close friend or family member.
- Expect them to say "yes" so that you won't fall off your chair or burst into tears when they do! Remember you are not asking someone who is an ice-cold stranger. You are giving them the opportunity to make the contribution they want to make. There is no need for you to beg, strong-arm, or cajole.
- When the person says yes, let them know you are really excited about their gift—that it means a great deal to you. You want to make this person feel truly wonderful about giving to your cause.

- Even if they say no, listen closely for the cues as to what they need next so you can be sure they get that before you ask them again. You want to leave this person looking forward to seeing you the next time, so that when they finally do say yes, they will feel great about it.

You will see that asking someone for money can be serious or playful, short and to the point, or long and drawn out. No two Asks are ever the same, because no two people are the same. The zone you are aiming for is a playful, listening, friendly give-and-take, always with a strong commitment to the result. And the more fun you can have with the process, the better.

CHAPTER 26

HONOR YOUR DONORS

Most donors don't need plaques or expensive recognition events put on just for them. They would rather know how much of a difference their contribution allows you to make. So invite them to be your special guests at events that highlight your results—the results their support made possible.

Set a goal of having each Multiple-Year Donor attend two of these events each year. Then make sure you inspire them so they leave the event saying, "I'm glad I give money here. I will keep doing that. Maybe I could give more."

For example, if one of your teachers just won a national award or your group of kids is going to graduate, invite your donors to attend the ceremony. You may have an upcoming art show of your participants' art, a reunion of all the babies born in your hospital in a given year, or a forum with a sought-after speaker in your field. By having these events underwritten or sponsored and adding a special reception with a ten to fifteen minute program just for your Multiple-Year Donors, they become a great opportunity to connect with and acknowledge your donors.

These events are also a way for your donors to introduce others to your work. Welcome them to invite their friends and family to join them to learn more about the organization, and be sure to make it clear that this is a free event where nobody will be asked for money.

The program part of the special reception for donors and their guests should include:

- A welcome and thank you from a board member.
- A talk from your organization's Visionary Leader highlighting the programs and services made possible by private contributions as well as the dreams of the organization or program.
- A live testimonial or video showcasing someone whose life has been changed thanks to your program.

In addition to the formal program element, give your donors plenty of time to mix and mingle. The networking effect of these events is magical. Be sure the crowd is interspersed with people who can give you feedback the next day. Also be sure to follow up with each donor individually to thank them for coming and to get their feedback about the event.

You will find that these events not only honor your donors, they keep them connected to their passion for your work and deepen their relationship to your organization.

THE JOY OF FUNDRAISING— TRUE CONTRIBUTION

As you shift your thinking, focus, and actions from a context of scarcity to one of abundance, you will begin to relax and let your own passion for the mission come through.

Your donors will feel so connected to your work that, rather than giving you a one-time donation to get you off their backs, they will take pleasure in making a true contribution. Your goal is to have each donor feel as though they have sprinkled fairy dust on the most worthwhile cause in the world—as if their gift to your organization is a personal indulgence for them.

After you receive each gift, let that donor know how excited you are and the difference their gift will make. Then you've made a real friend. You've allowed them to truly contribute to your organization and to feel the way you feel when you've truly contributed.

Then, and only then, will you know the true joy of fundraising.

RESOURCES FOR SUSTAINABILITY

For more information about the training and coaching programs offered by Benevon (formerly Raising More Money) to build sustainable funding for your favorite nonprofit organization, please visit www.benevon.com.

ABOUT THE AUTHOR

Terry Axelrod, CEO and Founder of Benevon (formerly Raising More Money), trains and coaches nonprofit organizations to implement a mission-based system for raising sustainable funding from individual donors. This system ends the suffering about fundraising and builds passionate and committed lifelong donors.

With over thirty years of experience in the nonprofit field, Axelrod has founded three nonprofits in the fields of health care and affordable housing. She realized early in her career that the only path to sustainable funding was to systematically connect donors to the mission of the organization, then involve and cultivate them until they were clearly ready to give—in short, to treat donors the way you would treat a close friend or family member, someone with whom you planned to have a lifelong relationship.

Axelrod created the Benevon Model in 1996 after serving as Development Consultant to Zion Preparatory academy, an inner-city Christian academy in Seattle, from 1992-1995. There she designed and implemented fundraising and marketing programs which yielded

$7.2 million in 2 ½ years as well as national recognition of the program, including a cover story in *The Chronicle of Philanthropy*.

Author of three previous books, *Raising More Money—A Step-by-Step Guide to Building Lifelong Donors*, *Raising More Money—The Point of Entry Handbook*, and *Raising More Money—The Ask Event Handbook*, Axelrod is also a sought-after speaker, both nationally and internationally. Her passionate commitment to the possibility of sustainable funding for all nonprofits drives the mission of Benevon and each of its programs. "The donors are truly out there—wanting to contribute; it's up to the organizations to connect donors powerfully to their work and nurture that connection over time. Our programs give each organization the tools to do that successfully."

Terry currently serves as a Director of the Giving Institute, a Trustee of the Greater Seattle Chamber of Commerce, and Life Trustee of Swedish Medical Center. She received her Master's of Social Work and Bachelor's Degrees at the University of Michigan, and she resides in Seattle with her husband, Alan, and their two children.